&

The 9 Strategies of WAR as a SUPERHERO

Amir Albaghdadi

ISBN:979-8-3304-1829-9

ISBN: 979-8-3304-1829-9

SIGMA MALE

THE LONE WOLF

& THE 9 Strategies of

WAR

As a SUPERHERO

PART ONE

SIGMA MALE

THE LONE WOLF

Introduction

What is the meaning of Sigma Mentality?

While growing up and interacting with other people Amir found himself lost in them all, it felt like he was different and he did not belong anywhere except maybe in a puzzle as the missing piece.

Although all of his friends struggled for attention, or simply imitated the actions of their peers, Amir preferred to stay by himself. He exchanged all the worldly approval for the things he loved; reading, long strolls in the nature, and freedom to be creative.

Little was he aware that he was part of Sigma fraternity; he was not an Alpha who hanker for attention or a Beta who join the band wagon.

This story plots the journey of Amir from where the Sigma way helped him to create a life of independence, and discovery untethered to social norms.

Chapter 1:

The Sigma Archetype vs. Alphas and Betas

In middle school, especially between young boys, there is this prominent group called 'the sigma' composed of the most popular and attractive students in school that play all the significant roles in school.

In this story Amir learned the hard way how much of an outsider he was from the rest of the population. While Alphas walked and talked confidently asserting their dominance over other children in on what games to play and who is cool the Betas followed them seamlessly.

Amir did not want to be a director and was not willing to be a follower; he wanted to be on his own. During lunch, while everybody talked loudly, Amir chose a place where he found him which is to be by himself. And, of course, dreamed. He did not feel lonely they were never encouraged and nor did he need the approval of others. To the contrary, what is important for Amir was to remain alone and enjoy the independence that he had got.

Chapter 2:

Sigma Mindset: Measuring Seven Fundamental Attributes

At this time, as Amir got to high school, he got a glimpse into many of these Sigma male characteristics. To help him gain his freedom, power, and assertiveness together with resourceful thinking became the hallmarks.

He had no strings attached with people and it was his self esteem that grew and bloomed. As his friends fommed gangs and hopped from one group to another in for the feel of acceptance, there was Amir going his own way, accepting the things other children would not consider doing.

He stumbled at one or two instances but I think he took these as lessons and challenges.

Chapter 3:

Embracing Solitude but not loneliness

There are times in the movie and in the novel when the main protagonist, Amir would be asked about his favorite moments in his life, and he would answer simply that he likes being alone. Remaining conscious of the effect of the technology on children of his generation, Amir was alone more often than not, roaming through the woods and thinking.

Time spent on the bank of the creek either reading or writing made him appreciate how important it was for one to be alone.

Amir loved his privacy but he ensured that he had friends with whom he enjoyed their company and not friends that were forced by the society.

Chapter 4:

Independence: The Road to Mastery,

High School proved that the independence of Amir was the powerful weapon. He took full ownership for his learning not as how to play a guitar but as in mastering computer skills which he knew would be useful in the future. Every day he spends time learning programming languages, watching tutorials, taking online classes, and working on projects in the bid to overcoming the world that engulfs the digital world.

With darkness settling and-literally- the horizon of the possibilities now starting to open, Amir spent hours in front of his computer screen, a passionate explorer. Unlike most students, who ask tutors or a fellow student to help them solve their homework, Amir was content with the challenge of teaching himself.

He waded through different coding languages, deconstructed software frameworks, and solving the challenges of design, and over time earned himself a fairly strong resume that was as satisfying as it was demanding.

His evenings were the combinations of experimentation now and then and the thirst for acquiring knowledge. Every bug fixed in the source code or the first website built was stepping stones towards the exciting universe of technology for him.

That is when the friends told other friends about the growing brilliance of the young student and the teachers who discovered his self-motivated learning.

Thus, the novel through the character of Amir, brilliantly depicts how later on, with determination and perseverance one can discover what lies inside of him.

He found out that he was not only becoming more skilled as he went through the experience of independent learning but was also becoming a better person, who is defined by confidence and readiness to tackle any problem that might come his way. This line comes at the climax of the chapter where Amir comes to a conclusion that this kind of journey was more important for him than any kind of academic lessons – such journey determined his further life and opened doors to the opportunities he had never even dared to dream about.

As Amir presses the keys on the keyboard or inputs a line of code, he started to build his own way to excel and finally got his independence and commitment to be free from any dependency to be able to achieve his goal.

Chapter 5:

Developing Emotional Independence

From the case of the film Amir stood out from other
kids in school for having never been emotionally
dependent on anyone.

Where all the other students were in search of approval
from outside world, the young man inside Amir was
fighting and getting strength from inside him.

Sometimes they bullied him about what he likes and
the things he does but all he has to do is laugh because
it doesn't change who he is. Emotional resilience arose
to be his shield with which he continued pressing on
regardless of what people said.

Chapter 6:

The Art of Social Mastery

Although Amir was not an anti-social person he knew how to make friends but in a different manner. Many boys at the school tried to conform to expectations, but Amir did not change his behavior.

He did not conform to this trend whether or the other but wore what suited him. This authenticity made people to be attracted to him.

What this means is that Sigmas like Amir can easily make and build on the relationships without compromising on their identity.

Chapter 7

Leadership Series: Working on Your Own Terms

Within An incredible leadership potential was hidden in Amir. He wasn't like an Alpha and barked out orders; he was a leader and acted as such.

In group projects, the performance was Keep up the hard work, and don't get too stressed out. People gravitated towards him, and this is due to embracing the qualities that are natural to him including the integrity and reliability.

Amir was able to prove to the readers that the true essence of leadership is not in making people perform certain action through the use of authority.

Chapter 8:

Debunking the Myths of the Sigma Personality

There occurred a number of misconceptions
about Amir, for instance being a loner.

In fact, he had unique bonds that he valued highly
and ensured he stay connected with a few close
people.

Some felt that Sigmas were unfriendly or probably
had Asperger's, but Amir was always keen on the
fact that he preferred working in a team though he
was an independent person who encouraged
others to improve.

Chapter 9:

Success Without Seeking Approval

The most admirable aspect of enshrinement of the particular success paradigm in the show is that Amir did not have to get anyone's approval for his healthy choices that led to developing muscles.

At the school talent show he did not look to gain praise but what he gained to feel was the achievement of just dancing.

His joy was not in clapping, but in achieving these goals- this is true testament of Sigmas not seeking validation from the public or in general, but achieving their personal feats.

Chapter 10:

Living by Your Own Code

With the university graduation looming, Amir was, once again, in front of great decisions. While others might had succumb to the various societal norms, Amir stood firm.

Nevertheless, he was focused on the things that mattered in his view – creativity, self development and genuine occupations of the future.

This means that Amir finally understood that all successes are achieved by being oneself and not following what is required in the society.

Conclusion:

The story of Destiny as Amir graduated and realized that he was a Sigma. That is the guide for other people: to be trustful and rely only on themselves, not to isolate themselves from friends while also not losing their aim.

Any person can leverage Sigma's potential and it begins with accepting diversity, embracing talents, and pursuing one's dream way to leadership. The key to the ability to make your own future is in your hands!

PART TWO

**THE 9
Strategies
of**

W
A
R

**As a
SUPERHERO**

DISCLAIMER:

The terms and concepts presented in this book are intended for entertainment purposes only. The references to "dummies" are used humorously and should not be taken literally or as a judgment of any individual's intelligence or character. The strategies and dialogues included are fictional and meant to add a light-hearted, playful tone to social interactions. They are not to be used as a serious guide to interpersonal communication or psychological assessment.

The content of this book is crafted to inspire creativity, humor, and self-confidence. It aims to encourage readers to approach life with a sense of fun and to handle social situations with grace and wit. However, it is essential to approach every individual with respect, kindness, and empathy in real-life interactions. Please note that the references to characters like Batman are purely for illustrative purposes and are not endorsed by or affiliated with any official Batman trademarks or entities. The book should be enjoyed as a work of creative fiction and not as a source of factual advice.

By reading this book, you acknowledge that the authors and publishers are not responsible for any actions taken or not taken based on the content provided. Enjoy the journey, embrace your inner superhero, and remember to approach every interaction with a smile and an open heart.

INTRODUCTION

Unfortunately, in these times, we are constantly surrounded by individuals who might not be as enlightened. Therefore, not everyone deserves to witness the full extent of your intelligence.

Once encountered by "dummies," here's how to verify and handle them with grace and humor:

How to Verify a Dummy?
As a superhero and the main character of your own epic story, you naturally attract attention. When a "dummy" approaches, they will instantly start asking intrusive questions about your personal life, occupation, and more. This behavior is a valid confirmation of a dummy.

How Do We Respond to a Dummy?
Once a dummy is confirmed, respond with a smile. The dummy might assume this smile is for them, but in reality, it's for your subconscious mind, affirming that you are steps ahead.

Here's how to handle the situation with elegance and a touch of Batman-esque mystery:
Hide Your Power: Don't reveal too much. Lead the conversation to a subject you enjoy, like your favorite superhero – Batman, for instance.
Engage with Humor: Share amusing anecdotes about Batman.

While the dummy collects data about a fictional
character, you are gathering real insights about them.
Stay Ahead: Keep the conversation light-hearted.
Remember,
you are the main character, and this is just another scene in
your grand narrative.

Reflect and Learn: Every encounter is an opportunity to
refine your strategies. Use these interactions to sharpen your
skills.

Inspire with Wisdom and Wit
In every interaction, maintain your poise and humor. Here's
a light-hearted script for such encounters:
Dummy: "So, what do you do for a living?"
You: "Oh, I moonlight as Batman. It's a tough job, but
someone's got to keep Gotham safe. How about you?"
This approach ensures you stay in control, keep the
conversation enjoyable, and gather the information you need

without revealing too much.

Remember, being the main character means you navigate
through life with confidence, strategy, and a sense of humor.

Following are THE 9 Strategies of WAR As a SUPERHERO!

STRATEGY No. 1

Be the Main Character

Embrace your role as the protagonist in your own life story. Just as Batman takes center stage in Gotham, you must step into the spotlight of your own narrative. This means being confident, assertive, and aware of your surroundings. Every decision you make should align with your personal mission and values. Own your story, and let your actions reflect the hero within you.

Be a Superhero

Adopt the mindset of a superhero. This involves more than just having a strong moral compass; it means developing resilience, courage, and the ability to inspire those around you. A true superhero is not defined by their powers but by their unwavering commitment to justice and the greater good. In your daily life, strive to be a beacon of hope and positivity, making choices that elevate not only yourself but also those you encounter.

Understand Your Nemesis

Just as every superhero has a nemesis, you too will face challenges and adversaries. Understanding your nemesis is crucial. Whether it's a difficult situation, a personal fear, or an actual person, recognize what you're up against. Study their tactics, anticipate their moves, and develop strategies to counteract them. Knowledge is your greatest weapon.

Build Your Team

No superhero fights alone. Assemble a team of trusted allies who complement your strengths and compensate for your weaknesses. This could be friends, family, colleagues, or mentors. These people will support you, provide different perspectives, and help you achieve your goals. Remember, even Batman has his Bat Family.

Train Relentlessly

Heroes are made, not born. Invest time in honing your skills, both mental and physical. Continuous learning and self-improvement are non-negotiable. Whether it's taking up a new hobby, advancing in your career, or maintaining physical fitness, relentless training ensures you're always ready for the battles ahead.

Harness Your Resources

Like Batman's utility belt, your resources are tools that can help you navigate through life's challenges. This includes your knowledge, skills, financial assets, and network. Be resourceful and innovative in using what you have at your disposal. Leverage technology, seek out new opportunities, and always have a plan B.

Adapt and Overcome

Flexibility is key in any battle. Situations change, and so must you. Adaptability allows you to pivot when faced with unexpected obstacles. Stay calm, assess the new landscape, and adjust your strategy accordingly. The ability to overcome adversity is what separates heroes from the rest.

Inspire Others

A true superhero inspires those around them. Lead by example and use your actions to motivate and uplift others. Share your knowledge, offer support, and be a source of encouragement. When people see the hero in you, they'll be inspired to find their own inner strength.

Reflece legendary!

Reflect and Grow
After every battle, take time to reflect on what you've learned. Analyze your successes and failures, and use these insights to grow stronger. Personal growth is a continuous journey, and each experience is a stepping stone toward becoming a better version of yourself. Embrace the process and celebrate your progress.

By integrating these strategies into your life, you embody the essence of a superhero. You become the main character in your epic story, navigating through challenges with confidence, wisdom, and a touch of humor, just like the Dark Knight himself. So, don your metaphorical cape, and let your adventures be legendary!

STRATEGY
No. 2

Warrior Mindset

Islam, as a comprehensive way of life, offers profound insights and guidance that can strengthen and empower individuals, especially when adopting a warrior mindset. This spiritual and mental fortitude has been exemplified by notable figures such as Muhammad Ali, Malcolm X, and Andrew Tate, who drew inspiration from their faith to overcome adversities and achieve greatness.

The Power of Faith in Empowerment
Warrior Mindset

Muhammad Ali: Known as "The Greatest Boxer," Muhammad Ali's conversion to Islam was a pivotal moment in his life. Embracing Islam provided him with a sense of purpose and an unwavering belief in himself. Ali famously said, "I am the greatest, I said that even before I knew I was." His faith instilled in him the courage to stand against racial injustice and the resilience to reclaim his heavyweight title after being stripped of it for his refusal to be drafted into the Vietnam War. Ali's warrior mindset was not just about physical prowess but also about moral and spiritual strength, derived from his faith in Islam.

Self-Reflection and Growth

Malcolm X: Initially a member of the Nation of Islam, Malcolm X later embraced Sunni Islam after his pilgrimage to Mecca. This transformation was profound, shifting his perspective on race and unity. Islam taught him the importance of self-reflection and growth. Malcolm X's journey from a troubled youth to a prominent civil rights leader is a testament to how Islam can guide individuals toward personal and social transformation. His famous quote, "If you have no critics, you'll likely have no success," reflects the resilience and introspection that his faith fostered.

Discipline and Focus

Andrew Tate: Although controversial, Andrew Tate has spoken about the discipline and focus that Islam has brought into his life. The religion's emphasis on regular prayer, fasting, and self-control aligns with the principles of a warrior mindset. By following these practices, Tate has found greater clarity and purpose, enabling him to pursue his goals with relentless determination.
Strategic Empowerment through Islamic Teachings

Trust in Divine Wisdom: Like a seasoned general trusts in battle strategies, a believer trusts in Allah's plan. This trust empowers individuals to face challenges with confidence and serenity.
Patience and Perseverance: Islam teaches that patience is a virtue. The Quran mentions, "Indeed, Allah is with the patient" (Quran 2:153). This principle is crucial for maintaining a warrior mindset, as it encourages enduring hardships with grace and steadfastness.

Community and Brotherhood: The concept of Ummah, or community, in Islam, fosters a sense of belonging and mutual support. This collective strength is essential in navigating life's battles, knowing that one is never alone.

Moral Integrity: Upholding justice and righteousness is a key tenet of Islam. This moral compass ensures that one's actions, even in conflict, are guided by ethical principles, much like a warrior who fights with honor.

Continuous Learning: Islam encourages the pursuit of knowledge. This principle is akin to refining one's strategies in war. By continuously learning and adapting, a believer remains sharp and prepared for any challenge.

Example Interaction Inspired by Faith
Inquisitive Person: "So, what drives you to keep pushing forward?"
You: "My faith in Islam teaches me that every challenge is a test and an opportunity for growth. Like Muhammad Ali once said, 'He who is not courageous enough to take risks will accomplish nothing in life.'"

By integrating these Islamic principles into your life, you can develop a powerful warrior mindset, staying true to your values while navigating the complexities of the modern world. Just as Muhammad Ali, Malcolm X, and Andrew Tate used their faith to empower themselves, you too can harness the strength of Islam to lead a life of purpose, resilience, and triumph.

STRATEGY
No. 3

Follow the Law and Use It to Your Advantage

In the grand theater of life, much like a strategic battleground, the law serves as both a shield and a sword. To navigate this landscape effectively, one must understand the rules and leverage them to their benefit.

This isn't about manipulation; it's about strategic thinking and maximizing opportunities within the boundaries of fairness and justice.

Understanding the Law

Just as Batman abides by his own moral code while fighting crime in Gotham, you too must be well-versed in the laws that govern your world. Knowledge is power, and understanding the legal frameworks can help you make informed decisions, protect your interests, and even turn potential obstacles into stepping stones.

Applying the Law Strategically

Once you comprehend the legal landscape, you can begin to use it to your advantage.

Here are a few ways to do this:

Protect Your Rights: Ensure that your rights are always safeguarded. Know what you are entitled to and stand firm in protecting your interests.

Utilize Legal Resources: Whether it's through contracts, agreements, or advisories, use legal tools to secure your position and advance your goals. This could mean anything from securing intellectual property to negotiating favorable terms in a business deal.

Stay Informed: Laws change, and staying updated ensures you are never caught off guard. Regularly review relevant legal updates and consult with professionals when necessary.

Examples of Strategic Legal Use

In Business: When negotiating a contract, ensure that all terms are clear and beneficial. Use clauses and stipulations that protect your interests and provide flexibility.

In Personal Matters: Understanding family law can help you navigate complex situations like inheritance, custody, or even prenuptial agreements with a clear head and a firm grasp on what's fair and just.

Reflect and Adapt
Every encounter with the law is a learning experience. Reflect on these experiences to refine your strategies. Just as every battle teaches a warrior about their strengths and weaknesses, every interaction with the legal system can offer insights into how to better protect and advance your position in the future

War Strategy in Daily Life

Applying war strategies to everyday life doesn't mean constant conflict; it means being prepared, strategic, and wise. Follow the law, use it to your advantage, and let it be one of the many tools in your arsenal as you navigate through your epic story. Be like Batman—vigilant, knowledgeable, and always a step ahead.

By embracing these strategies, you ensure that you are not just surviving but thriving, turning every challenge into an opportunity, and every interaction into a step towards your grand narrative. So, go forth with the wisdom of a seasoned warrior and the heart of a hero, and may your journey be as legendary as the tales of the Dark Knight!

STRATEGY
No. 4

Reputation

In the grand theater of life, reputation is your most valuable asset, functioning as both a shield and a sword. It precedes you, shaping perceptions and opening doors long before you utter a single word. As with any great warrior or superhero, your reputation is forged through your actions, decisions, and the way you handle those inevitable encounters with "dummies."

Building and maintaining a stellar reputation requires a strategic approach, much like the maneuvers in a well-fought war.

Here's how to cultivate and wield your reputation with the finesse of a seasoned general:

Consistency is Key: Just as Batman remains a steadfast protector of Gotham, ensure that your actions are consistent with your values and principles. Consistency builds trust and reliability, crucial components of a solid reputation.

Integrity: Uphold integrity in all your dealings. Whether in personal or professional interactions, honesty and ethical behavior will solidify your standing as a person of character.

Remember, even in the face of "dummies," maintaining your integrity showcases your strength.

Visibility: Make your positive actions visible to others. Share your accomplishments and good deeds, not boastfully, but humbly. Let others see the superhero within you, inspiring them with your example.

Adaptability: Be adaptable, like a skilled warrior who can adjust tactics on the battlefield. Show that you can thrive in various situations, always rising to the occasion with grace and competence.

Empathy and Understanding: Develop a reputation for being empathetic and understanding. People will remember how you made them feel more than what you said. Engaging with kindness, even with "dummies," enhances your reputation as a compassionate and wise individual.

Professionalism: In your career, maintain a high level of professionalism. Meet deadlines, deliver quality work, and communicate effectively. Your professional reputation will pave the way for opportunities and alliances.

Resilience: Demonstrate resilience in the face of adversity. Like Batman facing his villains, show that you can overcome challenges without losing your composure. Your ability to bounce back will earn you respect and admiration.

Innovation: Be known for your creativity and innovative solutions. Share new ideas and approaches, positioning yourself as a forward-thinker and a problem-solver.

Network Wisely: Build and maintain a network of respected individuals. Your reputation is often influenced by the company you keep. Surround yourself with people who uplift and inspire you.

In conclusion, reputation is a powerful tool in your arsenal. It reflects your essence and guides others' perceptions of you. By managing it with wisdom, wit, and unwavering integrity, you can navigate through life's challenges and triumphs like the legendary Dark Knight. So, go forth and let your reputation be as formidable as Batman's, illuminating your path and inspiring others along the way.

STRATEGY
No. 5

Self-Awareness

Self-awareness is the cornerstone of any successful strategy, whether on the battlefield or in the complexities of daily life. As a human, understanding your own strengths and weaknesses, motivations, and emotions is essential to navigate through challenges with the precision and confidence of a seasoned warrior.

Knowing Thyself
The ancient adage "know thyself" holds profound wisdom. Being self-aware means having a deep understanding of your own identity, values, and goals. It requires honest introspection and the courage to face your true self, including the shadows and imperfections that make you uniquely you.

The Power of Reflection
Take time to reflect on your experiences, decisions, and actions. Analyze what drives you, what fears hold you back, and what passions propel you forward. This reflection will equip you with the knowledge to make informed decisions and to respond to situations with clarity and purpose.

Emotional Intelligence
Self-awareness also encompasses emotional intelligence. Recognize your emotions and understand their impact on your thoughts and behaviors. By managing your emotions effectively, you can maintain composure under pressure, communicate more effectively, and build stronger relationships.

Adapting to Change
In the ever-changing landscape of life, adaptability is key. A self-aware individual is not rigid but fluid, capable of adjusting strategies and approaches to meet evolving circumstances. This flexibility allows you to stay ahead, much like a skilled general who adjusts tactics based on the unfolding dynamics of the battlefield.

Leveraging Strengths and Addressing Weaknesses
Identify your strengths and leverage them to your advantage. Whether it's your intellect, creativity, or resilience, use these attributes to achieve your goals. Simultaneously, acknowledge your weaknesses and seek opportunities for growth and improvement. This balanced approach ensures you are well-rounded and prepared for any challenge.

Mindfulness Practices
Incorporate mindfulness practices into your routine to enhance self-awareness. Techniques such as meditation, journaling, and mindful breathing can help you stay grounded and present. These practices foster a deeper connection with yourself and enable you to respond to life's demands with greater calm and insight.

Strategic Self-Improvement
Consider self-awareness as a lifelong journey. Continuously seek knowledge, challenge your assumptions, and embrace new experiences. Each step forward in self-awareness is a step toward becoming the best version of yourself, capable of leading with wisdom and authenticity.

In conclusion
In the grand narrative of your life, self-awareness is your most powerful ally. It is the foundation upon which all other strategies are built. By understanding and embracing your true self, you navigate through life's battles with the grace and cunning of a legendary warrior. So, harness the power of self-awareness, and let it guide you toward a future filled with purpose, resilience, and endless possibilities.

STRATEGY
No. 6

Recognize Potential Threats

Just as Batman surveys Gotham with a watchful eye, you must remain vigilant and aware of potential threats in your life.

This strategy is not about paranoia, but about being prepared and proactive. Recognizing a potential threat early allows you to navigate situations with foresight and wisdom, ensuring you remain steps ahead, just as the Dark Knight does. Here's how to implement this strategy effectively:
Stay Observant: Like a detective,

pay attention to your surroundings and the people in them. Notice body language, tone of voice, and actions. These subtle cues can often be the first indicators of a potential threat.

Gather Information: Use your interactions to collect data. Engage in conversations and listen more than you speak. The more you know about your environment and the people within it, the better you can anticipate and mitigate risks.

Trust Your Instincts: Your intuition is a powerful tool. If something feels off, it probably is. Trust your gut feelings and investigate further when necessary.
Stay Prepared: Have a plan in place for various scenarios. Whether it's a difficult conversation, a challenging work situation, or a personal conflict, knowing how you will respond can give you confidence and control.
Build Alliances: Just as Batman has allies like Robin and Commissioner Gordon, build your network of trusted friends and colleagues. These allies can provide support, advice, and assistance when threats arise.

Learn and Adapt: After each encounter, take time to reflect on what you learned and how you can improve. Every experience is an opportunity to refine your strategies and become more adept at recognizing and handling potential threats.
By embracing these practices, you will navigate through life with the same preparedness and keen awareness as a superhero. Remember, the goal is not to live in fear but to empower yourself with the knowledge and skills to handle whatever comes your way with grace and confidence.

STRATEGY
No. 7

The Art of War

Building on the foundation of handling dummies with grace and humor, it's essential to delve deeper into the strategies that can elevate your interactions and ensure you navigate your life like a true superhero. Here are nine strategies of war, adapted for the modern-day human:

1. Collect Information Data
Just as a general gather intelligence before a battle, you must collect data in your everyday encounters. Information is power, and understanding the motives, interests, and behaviors of those around you can give you a tactical advantage. Observe, listen, and learn – every detail can be a piece of the puzzle.

2. Know Your Terrain
In any encounter, knowing your environment can be incredibly advantageous. Whether it's a social gathering, a workplace, or a casual meetup, familiarize yourself with the setting. This will help you maneuver conversations and situations to your benefit, maintaining control and confidence.

3. Anticipate Moves

Like a chess master, think several steps ahead. Predict the questions and comments that might come your way and prepare witty, engaging responses. This foresight will keep you calm and collected, no matter the situation.

4. Use Psychological Warfare

Engage in subtle psychological tactics to influence and manage interactions. This doesn't mean manipulation, but rather an understanding of human psychology to foster positive and productive exchanges. Use humor, empathy, and keen insight to steer conversations in a favorable direction.

5. Maintain Flexibility

Flexibility is key in dynamic situations. Be ready to adapt your strategy as needed. If a conversation takes an unexpected turn, don't panic. Instead, pivot gracefully and use the new direction to your advantage, showing your versatility and resilience.

6. Build Alliances

In any scenario, allies can be invaluable. Form genuine connections and build a network of supportive individuals. These alliances can provide you with insights, resources, and backup when needed, enhancing your overall strategy.

7. Disguise Your Intentions

Just as you hide your powers from dummies, keep your true intentions close to your chest. Let others see what you want them to see while quietly working towards your goals. This mystery not only protects your plans but also adds to your intrigue.

8. Exploit Opportunities
Be vigilant and seize opportunities as they arise.
Whether it's a chance to showcase your skills, form a
new alliance, or gain valuable information, recognize
and capitalize on these moments. Being proactive
ensures you stay ahead in your grand narrative.

9. Reflect and Refine
After every interaction, take time to reflect on what
you learned and how you can improve. Continuous
self-assessment and refinement of your strategies
keep you sharp and prepared for future encounters.
Every experience, whether a triumph or a setback, is a
stepping stone to greater wisdom and capability.

By incorporating these nine strategies into your daily
life, you not only enhance your interactions but also
fortify your position as the main character in your
story. Navigate through life with the confidence,
strategy, and humor befitting a true superhero. And
remember, every encounter is another chapter in
your epic tale – make it legendary!

STRATEGY
No. 8

Engage in Wars, Not Battles

In the grand tapestry of life, it's essential to distinguish between skirmishes and significant campaigns. As the main character of your epic story, you must focus on the overarching war – the long-term goals and values that define your journey – rather than getting bogged down by minor battles that drain your energy and divert your attention.

When you engage in wars, you think strategically, planning your moves meticulously and anticipating the ripple effects of your actions.

Here's how to apply this principle to your daily life: Identify Your Core Objectives: Understand what truly matters to you. Is it achieving career success, fostering meaningful relationships, or personal growth? Clarify your goals and let them guide your decisions.

Prioritize and Allocate Resources Wisely: Time, energy, and focus are your most valuable assets. Channel them towards endeavors that align with your long-term objectives rather than wasting them on trivial disputes or distractions.

Stay Resilient and Adaptable: Wars are long and unpredictable. There will be setbacks and unexpected challenges. Develop resilience and adaptability to navigate these obstacles without losing sight of your ultimate goals.

Learn from Every Encounter: Each interaction, whether with allies or "dummies," offers valuable lessons. Reflect on these experiences to refine your strategies and grow stronger.

By focusing on the bigger picture and engaging in wars rather than battles, you ensure that your efforts are meaningful and impactful. This approach empowers you to live with purpose, making each day a chapter in your epic saga.
With every step, you embody the wisdom and resilience of a true hero, navigating life's challenges with grace, humor, and unwavering determination. So march forth, strategize wisely, and let your legend unfold.

STRATEGY
No. 9

Emerge Victorious: Success is the Best Revenge

In the grand theater of life, there will be moments when you encounter adversaries, much like the "dummies" we discussed earlier. These encounters can range from minor annoyances to significant challenges. However, true power lies not in retaliation but in rising above, proving your worth, and achieving success despite the obstacles.

Master Your Craft
Just as Batman has perfected his skills, so should you. Invest time in honing your abilities, whether they be professional, personal, or creative. Excellence in your field will naturally set you apart and command respect.

Maintain Composure
In the face of provocation, remain calm and collected. Your composure will speak volumes about your strength of character and will often disarm those who seek to undermine **you.**

Focus on Your Goals
Stay laser-focused on your objectives. Let your ambition and drive propel you forward, leaving detractors in the dust. Remember, the best way to silence critics is through undeniable achievement.

Cultivate Resilience
Success rarely comes without setbacks. Develop resilience to bounce back from failures and continue pushing forward. Each setback is a stepping stone to your ultimate triumph.

Lead by Example
Inspire others through your actions. Demonstrate integrity, hard work, and perseverance. By leading by example, you not only advance your own success but also uplift those around you.

Embrace Humility
While it's important to acknowledge your achievements, remain humble. True success is recognized through the respect and admiration of others, not through self-aggrandizement.

Celebrate Your Victories
Finally, take the time to celebrate your accomplishments, no matter how small. Recognize the milestones on your journey and use them as motivation to continue striving for greatness.

In every battle, whether literal or metaphorical, the key to victory lies within you. By mastering your craft, maintaining composure, and focusing on your goals, you can achieve success and rise above any adversary. Remember, the greatest revenge is not in retaliation, but in living a life so full of achievement and joy that those who doubted you are left in awe. So, go forth with confidence, strategy, and a sense of humor, and let your victories be as legendary as the Dark Knight's.

THE 9
Strategies
of

W
A
R

As a
SUPERHERO

Special note:

Consider giving us your kind review.

Best wishes,

SUPERHERO
POWERS

Von
Amir
Albaghdadi